GREEN OF ALL HEADS

GREEN OF ALL HEADS

poems

---

aracelis girmay

AMERICAN POETS CONTINUUM SERIES NO. 215

BOA EDITIONS, LTD. * ROCHESTER, NY * 2025

First Edition
23 24 25 26 7 6 5 4 3 2 1

Publications by BOA Editions, Ltd.—a nonprofit corporation under section 501 (c) (3) of the United States Internal Revenue Code—are made possible with funds from a variety of sources, including public funds from the Literature Program of the National Endowment for the Arts; the New York State Council on the Arts, a state agency; and the County of Monroe, NY. Private funding sources include the Max and Marian Farash Charitable Foundation; the Mary S. Mulligan Charitable Trust; the Rochester Area Community Foundation; the Ames Amzalak Memorial Trust in memory of Henry Ames, Semon Amzalak, and Dan Amzalak; and contributions from many individuals nationwide. See Colophon on page 132 for special individual acknowledgments. Any use of this publication to "train" generative artificial intelligence (AI) technologies to generate text is expressly prohibited.

Cover Design: Sandy Knight
Cover Art: Valentina Améstica & Aracelis Girmay
Front Cover Concept and Original Font: Valentina Améstica
Interior Design and Composition: Isabella Madeira
BOA Logo: Mirko

BOA Editions books are available electronically through BookShare, an online distributor offering Large-Print, Braille, Multimedia Audio Book, and Dyslexic formats, as well as through e-readers that feature text to speech capabilities.

Cataloging-in-Publication Data is available from the Library of Congress.

BOA Editions, Ltd.
250 North Goodman Street, Suite 306
Rochester, NY 14607
www.boaeditions.org
A. Poulin, Jr., Founder (1938–1996)

CONTENTS

IV

V

*

DECEMBER

Or that I would run my hand along
the dip in the hill's grey back
up to its withers, feeling
the closeness of its heat,
its inwardness risen and risen and blown away

To be among their small group,
their mouths to the earth, their silences

Uncle is, swishing away the flies
Mother is, pouring black coffee through their hair

Each of us, briefly, a tense
cast into the other's time

Not to fill my ears with the sound of my own motion
but with ear

To hear the low voices of the shadows

To exist without the memory of words

To be traversed by elk, faces, wheels

To learn to stand outside the rooms of light

I

Abandon à soi, aux saisons, à la lune, au jour plus ou moins long. Cueillette. Et toujours et partout, dans les moindres représentations, primat de la plante, la plante piétinée mais vivace, morte, mais renaissante, la plante libre...

—Suzanne Césaire, "Malaise d'une civilization"
Tropiques 5, April 1942

Children
You were never meant to be human
You must be the grass
You must grow wildly over the graves

—Roger Reeves, from "Children Listen"

FUNERAL

There were velas where we sat in the chairs spirit to spirit with
the candles, the laying body of the deceased.

This is what I wanted for my father. To sit with him all day.
Death being death, but not that his body is over, I wanted to take
him home. To carry, like some people do, his body, his tunnels.
His bones.

His people do not believe in such things.
His people do not believe in burning the body to ashes.
He is not ours alone.

We called the Offices of Funerals. They were incorporated. All Rights Reserved. I asked them to please tell me as much as they could about the political backgrounds of the company owners. I considered the word "please" and how so much of this was out of our hands. *He had been taken out of our hands*. They were crossing the street. A teenager hit them. He killed them. Accidentally. They were killed. Having survived so much. Two maths, two friends, two fathers, two grandfathers. Adi. Adi. Beauty of the heart.

My brother was the one at the coroner's. Our father's body in their custody. My brother was the one to say, yes, he is ours, though not in those words.

I had the phone to my head. I asked the Offices of Funerals, Please, what do your company's owners think about Trump. Are there flags in your office. Some trace of where all this money would go and how they would treat our father's body.

They charged us for every service. We gave them our dad's own money for the tools, the coffin, the room. They gave us a limit, a maximum number of people who could be present, because this death was not ours.

The flowers were pageant. Stiff, bright, extravagant.

Whose hands had cut and tied and pierced the living stems into the false, green foam. It was chemical. It was absurd.

Of all the ceremonies I have attended, I remember in Santurce the room of the rumbero. Through it death flew freely, swooping as a bat.

They had brought his death over the street. They had brought his death through the narrow doorway and into the bar where the bat flew dizzily, changing shape—death being death.

His coffin was a canoe. All of our bodies churned a sea. We wore yellow and red. We were meeting under a blackgreen tree. Among the people I come from are the people who rode canoes out of the sky onto the waters around this very island.

Everyone brought parts of the fish to make a soup and his body lay there as they played their drums and women stirred the heads and meat so that first he, then everyone, could sing.

My loved one brought me there. He was paying his respects. We offered ours in a plastic bag that shone around the fish like a veil.

Because this death was not mine, I stood a little outside. I watched. Time took our fins and eyes and clothes and carried them back into the muds.

Bones were tunnels.

I could not follow where they led.

Bones were tunnels. We stepped into the flowerless mud.

We wore fishes in the dark. The sun weighed on
our heads and all sound died in the long smoke of
the frankincense. Time did its work
so that when the green beetle landed
on my brother's hand and then crossed gently
onto my finger there was
no doubt.

We are the leaves in his hands now.

WHAT I HEARD INSIDE THAT DARK WAS MINE

was mine a scorpion, was mine my own braid's
mother, it skittered away   out of story

so turned my eye to what was mine,
the blessing of the clouds and adey who said
stay here with me

my own one's beautiful hands
square and soft and black of plums

was mine my brother the branch
to clean our teeth

sun of face on the mountain

was mine those days of with you
                                        being horses

gk

dad

Through the house I rolled the stones
sometimes so large, sometimes so small
I crawled with my breath to the ground
to roll them forward. Alone & done,
though sometimes came through
the screaming of my children
or the neighbor's piano upstairs.
There was sometimes a moment
when in a flash the sunlight shocked my eyes
& suddenly I saw so clearly the world
that we had trampled, me & my stones.
I drank of hours or sometimes the one of wind
or the cup of children. Then over me
like a cloud covering my faces anew, the courage
was gone. I was rolling the stones again
through the six rooms of our house.
Were they the sounds of bees
when Y. came through the door
telling me the signs? I wrote to S.:
Where does all that gentleness
& beauty & brilliance go?
She said: It does not go.
I pressed the sentence to my chest like
horse's hair. I lived in it.
There were roses in your hands
when I last saw you in your last shirt
of blue & white checkers. A page of
graph paper. A year, I sat at the window
& looked for the order of numbers.
I studied the building across the street
& occasionally a hand out
of the window, fixing the laundry,
the face of a young man

with the sun on, smoking—
green of your joy in Emba Derho,
green of our tears there though you are.

Ceremony for Remembering the Doorless World

October

where three we-horses mark ground,
turn snake our necks inside the guayla circle. My aranci,

—etan, childfox
out my fourth mouth, you drank

then the year went dark

& our own flowers & fires & what we thought we were

though, still, our faces opened to
the whooping of coyotes

at the canyon rim,
how they throw their voices out,

falling, starless veils of lace
over our still, black heads.

Awake I sit sentried with all my Sight
& the purple fennel musting after rain.
This hour

Become my canyon, become my bottom of the
world
listening for your breaths—to ward off nonbreath.

Parent, my son—My son,
a flicker barely

born. Already

withstand the blanched eye of our grief

One morning with our faces crying into
the arroyo it answers:
Once there were no doors.
No doors on earth, not a single one.

—so when I listen I
still hear you still kicking the ball,

laughing as you say the story of endurance.

& the women flutter
a flock of sound suddenly lifts,

they throw their voicebirds over the births

so we are three & simultaneous earths inside
your coil of fatherhair to which I press my ear to hear
the histories, then the bell

Then the whirl The whir
of doctors above your beds,
your noiseless struggle to be.

Stay.   *Say.*

You are my Heres & Furthers
Daddy, now I join the mothers

Remember, when you were a little boy
I used to hold you?

Right after Dad's stroke
I could not keep
A fact or
Sentence straight
Where to start a story
& which details were
The important ones
This was already my problem
But my challenge
Grew & grew
& was of, I think,
A different nature
& I hadn't really
Noticed until
In the office w/U.
I kept mixing up the pronouns
So obviously
& then correcting
Myself, it had become
An impediment, I thought,
To my continuing,
It had felt impossible,
I mean, to continue
My story, how
For "him" I said
"They," or said
My brother's name,
& then my son's,
& also sometimes
Instead of "Dad"
I said "I."
Mostly I was not confused
In my mind, I was picturing
The correct person
But another word would
Come instead
& this went on a long time,

Weeks, maybe even months,
& I began to develop
A theory that maybe the
Circuits of relation had
Begun to shift & so
Certain things about
How my dad was feeling
& doing & what
He needed had changed
& newly overlapped
With the ways of being
Of my other beloveds
& of course some
Of this had already been
True a long time,
But it was like I was now
Having to learn to see again
& was starting to see these echoes,
These likenesses, newly,
& so my own words
Followed this new
Circuitry of feeling,
Shifting somewhere inside us
So that when I meant to say
"He was born in Gondar,"
Instead I said "I"
& felt really, really embarrassed.
It was happening at work a lot
When people would ask a question
About how he was doing or
On the phone with doctors,
& I felt like these were symptoms
Of something I should be ashamed of
Somehow, but now, from this distance,
It is just so sad to feel what
Everyone was suddenly going through,
Mostly my dad, but also all of us,

& now he is in his death
& I have mostly not done that
In a while & when I think of it
I think now there was something
Very powerful, very much
About the truth of his dearness to us
& how already his energies
Were distributing across us
& what I thought was confusion was not.
I was born in Gondar We had so
many siblings Now so many of
him are gone.

When I come home they rush to me, the flies, and would take me, they would take me in their small arms if I were smaller, so fly this way, that way in joy, they welcome me. They kiss my face one two, they say, *Come in, come in. Sit at this table. Sit.* They hold one hand inside the other and say, *Eat.* They share the food, sit close to me, sit. As I chew they touch my hair, they touch their hands to my crumbs, joining me. The rim of my cup on which they perch. The milky lake above which. They ask for a story: *How does it begin? Before, I was a child,* and so on. My story goes on too long. I only want to look into their faces. The old one sits still, I sit with it, but the others busy themselves now with work and after the hour which maybe to them is a week, a month, I sleep in the room between the open window and the kitchen, dreaming though I were the Sierra, though I were their long lost sister, they understand that when I wake I will have to go. One helps me with my coat, another rides my shoulder to the train. *Come with me, come,* I say. *No, no,* it says, and waits with me there the rest whistling, touching my hair, though maybe these are its last seconds on earth in the light in the air is this love, though it is little, my errand, and for so little I left my house again.

I GO TO THE DENTIST

I am on laughing gas and crying again in the dentist's chair, thinking of how young they were, my dad and S. and all the LA people of Eritrea. They rented a dentist's office after hours on the weekend and used it as an organizing space while we children played in the brown leather chair, shiny and split, in the back, among the instruments. They held their meetings and, when everything was still so small, informational sessions and fund-raisers in the front. It was there I first remember my dad playing koboro. His smile so full that his eyes disappeared. His straight, sharp teeth.

I am not sure how I gained this fear. When I was little I had surgery to remove the extra tooth caught in the x-rays, horizontal like a door lintel across my two front teeth. The healing hurt though what I most remember were the stitches dangling like whiskers. Later, the impacted teeth, the extra bones, and crowding.

At my new dentist in California I am making an effort to live. I am trying not to wear my body down like a shoe. The laughing gas has made me brave. I am saying to my dentist and the assistant, Thank you for your kindness. And when my mouth is stuck open and he is asking, How are you doing? I put my hand on my chest and give him a thumbs up to say Thank you so much. Good.

At my first visit with him when, for the first time, I am in tears, I tell him I have some extra fear about dentists which is the real thing. But I do not tell him that I started my root canal on March 11th or 12th or something and days later we were in lockdown and that I wouldn't go back for the next part until after we had gone to bury my father and that for the first year when I woke from sleep you were always just beneath the surface of my skin as though a lake, and when I woke I woke from swimming with you in your death, like we did when I was small and on your back and we counted to three then arrowed through the water holding our breaths.

Decades later we were in your car, driving from that Afghan restaurant in the plaza on Artesia when things were getting bad, and you were thinking of the smaller organisms, I think, when you were marveling at how it seems it is in the nature of living things to go on living. I thought then that I would find this moment again if I were the one to keep on living after you, but that's not what gives me comfort now, what comforts me is to think of your teeth and how for weeks after you died I could not feel myself because parts of you had settled in my branches and I grew the new grey hair right in front and knew that you were sleeping there wrapped in your ghabi and my teeth, my chewing, when I ate, were not mine but yours so much that it made me weep to eat. I like to remember right now how sharp, how full of smiling. How clean and full of integrity your chewing and eating. How neat your plate and portions. How beautiful your effort for order. After the stroke, wiping your mouth every few bites. How formidable your intelligence. How gentle your voices when you said sorry. I did not say any of this to the dentist and do not say now, when he is asking if I am okay, that I am thinking of death, that I am thinking of Belkis Ayon's Sikán again, con el chivo, I am having a realization about her cloak and amulet and eyes. Other eyes were the problem. They looked too hard. They touched and scrutinized and said awful things. When Sikán carried the baby into that other realm and she was looking back, her eyes were shields to ward off what looked, what chased. And mine too I used this way. With you it was different. My privacy respected. I could turn my back and study anything I wanted.

I heard Eileen Myles in a poem say "when I die / the dream dies too / one bolt" and it surprises me still to feel the strange comfort of that. Though other you goes on, I want to like to wonder about what does get completed in death. A. was so little (or was it E.?) when he tried to comfort me by saying, about you, that at least you had gone through it so you wouldn't have to die again. I think you would have found that interesting, an idea to keep working on over the years as you did with each of us.

I do not tell the dentist or the assistant that the gas is putting wings on my feet though they know. What will happen next? Just that I am calm in my amberish procedure-glasses and my warm clothes, attended to with suctions and water. I am studying a rectangle of light.

I do not tell the dentist I am in Cairo with a few days of layover on my way to Asmara, looking into shop windows onto nothing I coveted though I remember in great detail a carpet bag and its shining brown handles. The light shines on it as though it is a theater of story. Reds and browns. I am eating ice cream in my mind. It is night, the street is busy and lit. There is barely any money in my wallet. Enough for my rough room, some meals, for toast and bread. But I am flush with looking, family awaiting me in Asmara, a cube of butter wrapped in gold paper.

All this as he works on my teeth, telling me turn closer, turn away. I was so afraid, but the dentist and assistant treat me well. I feel closer to memory, closer to you here, flying and coming back, slowly landing from the laughing gas. When they ask, I do not say that I am having realizations.

It is true, I thought I was only eyes and that this was always part of the problem, but my mother fed me and you heard my voice and it was Y. who was loyal and strong and A. who met me at the airport after the news, the shocks still moving through me as the taxi pulled us through the cardboard-colored blocks up Flatbush toward my neighborhood, and she told me the story of the beetle landing on your hand and you opening your palm flat for it to have a resting place, and eating the rest of your lunch like that, with one hand open for the beetle, and the other hand for feeding yourself. So much returns to me, as though I am on a train. A book left open in the snow. The poem of Nazim Hikmet writing the things he didn't know he loved. My eyes are closed but I am looking out of the window of myself and will never stop talking with you.

I want to tell you that if this poem makes even one fearful person go to the dentist, then I would feel a part of something so useful, but maybe it is you scribbling in me in this dentist's chair and you already know, which makes such sense that this would be your poem. Grapes in a garden. Our new feet climbing the stone-pocked steps to the apartment. How gently the assistant wipes my face.

gk

One hand on the horse's rear to let him know
I was coming around to clean his other hooves.
How we ate from a single plate.
How we shared the dream of animals.

So, *Wake*, I began to say, to my heart,
from other rooms where also I swept the floors
& set the angles straight. Heart heart, I moved
with its worn eye hanging inside me,

& wrote on the door in chalk:
To be sharp as arrows (not sorrows),
You are called to say. & to say it meant,
somehow: Awaken & touch this life

to the other days we lived. Backwards through
the door of the bottlebrush, I am coming.

—simultaneity—

ግርማይና

You were a beautiful story grown out of the earth.

Close your eyes, close your eyes. It is not time to know.

*

NOTES FOR A SOUND YOU WERE

gk

-- to learn from the poet, who,
It seems to me, having searched & searched
& found the words
Behind the gates, unlatched one after the other
& watched them run to an other energy.
Some violet, braying with vitality, some tired,
Strong, willing themselves toward the morning.
So in the lead's grey trace I pull your name
Out of my live hand
Trying to write the notes for a sound you were
That ran out of this life you have gone out of
So that I may follow you. Where?

We played the tape then -- death --
We turned the tape over

I felt briefly bright with your mother's eye
When I read your name on the sticker of your finished casket
It sobered me of grief one second
How wrong it was of rage I was
The font & code
Something I wasn't supposed to see
A corporate coffee-order receipt
To die in the U.S. industry

But her eye was a god it flashed in me as a flash of ice
Like in Asmara
It took you off
It had done it before
(Or should I say "she"? She had done it before.)
Not a sound I could make, not even human

Though my humanness was a part of it
A material point
A filament
Of time
Through which she surged

Stone by stone, I knew then,
Each of our heads
Built around a star.

Then death.

Then carry what can be carried unto another star.

*

II

ANSWERS TO YOUR DISAPPEARING QUESTION

yes, we will -- we have been trying -- for as long as you --

have been -- where -- in the air? -- do you suggest -- how will we --

know? -- mind -- the flowers -- mind -- where you step --

we suspect -- we are already -- walking right -- through

CHILDHOOD

In the apartment with the orange
shag carpet, is one long table
surrounded by chairs,
only four of them matching,
and cups and pitchers and food, and large,
silver plates for sharing, a pot,
a ladle, a child's small and noisy toy,
and all of it empty of people.
Everyone has rushed out hurriedly
in the middle. Somewhere,
that room exists still, floating
toward the sun. The meat
and grapes petrified with years.
The cloth bleached by light
persisting through the windows.
Now the rattling of plates, the clattering
of forks and spoons. Louder to us it calls
the nearer it gets to the end.
It is saying one last thing.

PERCEPTION MILK

There was a time I
thought everything
could be known—

Jesus's red words in our
mother's leather
Bible could tell me.

I was nine & ten &
copied every name
onto my papers,

each trace a wooden
knot. Each name a leaf,
a box.

I tried to make a tree
of descendants
Genesis down.

Weekends with him our dad
intervened gently, Who is
this Jesus?

But I believed in
the authority
of the book

& thought there was a paper
for every thing. I read
the encyclopedia

for any traces all
was related,
otherwise my expression

nearly soundless in
the company of strangers
& only did my voice

from its small egg burst when I
ran & with the others
opened my arms

in ballet & then
garage routines
to Janet, J.J. Fad,

in a voltage of girls. We
bared our necks
in volume. We shone

& grew hungry
& with my hunger I went
into my mother's things

to try to know her,
to find the broom &
what she kept.

So tiny the plastic,
turquoise box, inside
of which:

a sleeping scarab. These
tiny figurines,
after whom I try

to carve my word. Inside a
velvet case: one sharp
childtooth.

The scattering scab
of my brother's cord.
& curls. These drawers

out of which, still,
I lift my syntax eaten
by moths, their wooden view

of our faces & hands as
we hurried to glimpse
what was there, as if

opening, closing the beds
of time into which my
secret mother kept traces

& their powers, which
are the words
I long for, still.

The private words
of her drawers
& hair,

I tried
to drink
my milk

from there.

TRANSMISSION

In all the parks of our childhood, the coupling
of couples all flush, all long, all lost in
the other's mouth. Blankets—emerald & gold—
& families with shoulders all same-shaped bending
in & out of the cooler. Watermelon.
Aluminum foil over Styrofoam plates.
We watched. Peripheral, coyote,
momentarily unmothered. Our father
on the field, running. We stayed all day
emptying out of swings, & sand
from the sockets of our sobbing
shoes. Hot metal slide while people posed in
pictures at the bleached, blue fountain
& by roses if there were. Our laces, burred.
A psychic eye of silty ice flashing cold
beside the trash. Silver pistol. A can of Crush.
Then dusk came covered the African heads
of Asmara, Kingston, Birmingham.
Long blur of mariachi trying to touch.
By now, some, the loved ones, come coming in the static.
Dandelion the brother, the sister air
now. We know three names. Our dead are
arriving. By now arriving & hovering
    the black, yellow, green of the fruit of the radios.

We are all of us here because of war.

FAITH

Our Mother
wept over

the open
oven door

where she, a
candle, hid

her wild,
torn face

from us, it
must have been,

though we're not
in the scene

until swiftly
the pan and

her lighting
just one wick

to sing, by
then her face

all private,
all dry and

gold as
Spanish onion

whose skin, when
I cut, floats

to my wrist
far ahead

in the time
of my own

kitchen, gold I
bend to now

trying to
listen for

what faith
it was that,

washing
the dishes,

anointing
our heads,

planting way,
closing all light,

put its hand
inside Our

Mother's hand.

SIBLING

furcula

I

Lately my child is asking,
I was just daydreaming. Could you hear me?

But no, she is not making sounds that I can hear.
In this life.

A couple of years ago
when she was smaller, I
said "my comma," she
would ask her brother, I
dreamed about x or y or z,
do you remember?

Though it would seem same room, same
hour, same sleep, she could not
understand her dreams were not also his.

This drove him crazy.
I keep telling you, I can't see your dreams.
And we'd say, Okay, okay, she's learning, while
opening and shutting the cabinets in the
kitchen and warming the milk. Of almost
everything he has he gives her half.

There are so many ways to read these mornings
including this. We have lost so many things.
The people the children are and aren't like,
the ways of speaking that might
reach them.

I am taking this thought down the hill where
the yarrow and fennel grow everywhere.

What to give them for the stomach.
What to give them for the heart.

2

In the childhood stories my father told
the forest and the branches, soccer and the hills.

                        He was the third
of nine siblings, the first one who
died. Did they name herhim?

eyelashes

            and all the faint record beneath the stones.

His sister after him
stayed in the kitchen. She snuck food to their oldest
brother with whom she was in alliance but not to
my father with whom she was in a kind of
competition, they laughed hard about that as older people.

In the childhood stories my father told rocks
and trees and killing the smallest animals. It was Abraham
who would not fight, who would not point
the slingshot at the bird. When he was older,
in a political meeting in an old church I think it was,
the military came in shooting. His friends were killed
beside him and he fell with them, pretending to be dead.
It was Abraham who went to war and left The Front to bring
his siblings to Sudan and then went back.
It was Abraham who was killed.

We were in the car, I think,
one of the times my father told the story in that way
as though just realizing it for the first time. How Abraham
would not kill the bird.

To witness the whole life of another as children and then as
adults. To keep perceiving, inexhaustibly.

The brown splay of the rosemary's path inside the green bush
of itself.

The generations of its violet eyelet flowers on every street here,
rosemary uncle.

3

A sibling who is always there.
Nearly invisible. Ubiquitous.
With whom you shared a plate.
With whom you did and did not want to share
a song, a chair.

Who saw maybe so many of your
faces as was true of me and my own
brother who was in first grade, I think, when I first sensed
what I could and could not know. I was in fourth.
He glid through whole fields of radio lyrics
all filled up with himself, and on the school stage
led by the music teacher, sang all the words to
brown paper packages tied up with string
in that recital and it was amazing to me
that he had all that melody and language and speed.

He cut away then, like an eye,
to where I could not follow.
Suddenly his own wise thing.

4

For my mother, there were cousins first.
Then siblings to race and teach and run.

The roses of one sibling.
The quiet of another. The laughter of
the closest one.

One would know what to give for the heart.
One would know what to give for the stomach.

But in the biggest, longest book on my mother's shelf
is the story of a woman who trades three of her children for food
for the youngest one.

This one grew big and gold and when she
laughed, coins shook inside her like a rattle.

5

When Mom made me leave for that boarding school
she broke a bone so nevermind whose bone was it,

we could not fly.

But it is there I dream the lunch table of the long,
aluminum fact of our childhood.

I am pulling the parts of my lunch out
of a brown paper bag.

Handful after handful of grass and
all my friends recede.

My brother breaks his small dictionary in half
and gives it to me like bread when I thought I was alone.

YOUR WORDS AGAIN

K
WEARING A DRESS. SHE HANGS THE CLOTHES OUT TO DRY AND THIS FORMS TWO REALMS ON EITHER SIDE.

Z
THE LIVING ONE.

B
Z'S ELDER, NOW PASSED. A'S SIBLING.

A
Z'S OTHER ELDER, NOW PASSED. B'S SIBLING.

THE CARRIERS
TWO TO FOUR PEOPLE WHO CARRY THE LIVING TO THE OTHER SIDE OF THE WASH.

|
|
DEAD | LIVING
|
|
|

K enters through the side of the dead with a basket of clothes to dry. One by one, she hangs each item on the line with clothespins, straight down the middle of the field. Pants, shirts, a dress. She stays on the side of the dead, careful not to touch the other side. Maybe she is humming or reciting something to herself very quietly. When she is finished with this work she exits from where she came.

A and B are carried, each in a chair (as is done in wedding celebrations), by the carriers. They are carried from the side of the living to the side of the dead. They are facing away so that anyone watching can only see their backs. When they reach their places on the other side, the carriers face them forward. Whether they are carried in together or one in front of the other, desire to go or do not desire to go, depends entirely on A, B, and the carriers. This can be negotiated publicly or privately. The carriers then sit with A and B on the side of the dead, and A begins preparing coffee ceremony for everyone. From the moment A is seated, the coffee ceremony begins.

Z enters, without a chair, her movement intuitive and improvised. She must stay on the living side of the wash. She is cleaning her side of the space. Sweeping, folding, stacking things.

People on the side of the dead are talking about the weather, the news. Z is listening in, sometimes asking questions.

During coffee ceremony when A walks the roasted coffee around for everyone to smell, she sticks the pan through the divider/ clothesline in order for Z to smell it and to participate in coffee ceremony. She also serves Z coffee, never fully crossing the line or even looking her in the face.

Once everyone has their first round of coffee, finjal in hand, B exits and comes back with a radio. He pulls the antenna out and everything goes dark and then is bright again. Z begins to speak. It is the middle of a conversation. All conversation that happens must be negotiated through the laundry. They can reach through with legs, feet, arms, hands but can't see each other's faces through the clothes.

Z: Did I ever tell you that one? How we were trying to get out of the house, if we could just make it to the door. But we were so heavy with feathers.

There was also that one of the woman tearing bread from her stomach to feed us. Do you know who that was?

A/B/the carriers: [Silence. It's as if the connection is not entirely clear. Someone turns the dial of the radio, there is some static and then it is clear again.]

Z: Or when I was pregnant, was one of you the opossum who looked at me through the leaves?

I just remember thinking after you died that death was a problem to be solved, a threshold to withstand. As though it were something that could end.

A/B/the carriers: [Static]

Z: Have I lost your words again?

A: You were saying something. A string of dreams.

Z: Since you died, I can only point to what I wished I had been born to be, or to what I was meant to be but never was, and just the feeling that you knew which life I was supposed to live, which details, which choices. Like you had a sense of the track and how far I'd gone away from it, and what it would take to get the family back to some good place. Then with you went the point of reference.

A: [With pity] Gualey.

B: You wanted to scratch your gums and rub them with ash to make them black. And when we died you watched videos of monks in Debre Damo. [A is surprised.] There are skulls up there. It was so interesting that you were doing that. Why were you doing that?

Z: First you named me
Then you left me below a vast, blue sky
Open, as a fig

So I hid inside the trunk of a tree, and then the shells and skins of the animals

And then words

And then silence

I was old enough to walk but my brother was barely counting to 100.

B: [Silence]

Z: Are you there?

B: [Silence, turning the dial, then] I am here. It is just that... [tickled] you'll think this is funny... the connection is slow

Z: [She continues without hearing B] Can you hear me?

[Just hearing the joke] Amazing. [Waiting in silence to listen for what else might be heard.]

A: I know. You're trying to hear what he's going to say next but don't miss what else there is to hear, or forget what you yourself were going to say...

B: What were you saying?

Z: I guess, I think I was trying to say something about how it was also wordless there. And maybe how I'm still stuck there, trying to understand something. Or maybe just that I can't get over it. It's like nothing happened, and yet. Everything ended right in the beginning. There was a family, aunts, uncles, parents, places. And then, such serial catastrophes. And we were all just thrown out of those windows, into orbit, separately. I imagine you felt that much more acutely than we did.

I have been trying to listen in. I don't know why. Maybe out of loyalty. And there is not a single word, just sometimes the smallest thing speaking from the periphery, a trail of ants, a cotton cloth folded for a day that would not come. It's like I'm somewhere I was never supposed to be.

B: In the beginning, no one tells us how hard it will be. You are born and most times there is such happiness. There should be arms and words to greet the baby depending on what the child is born into. But there is nothing like this part of it. It takes some time, honeyey. But already it has been a long time.

A: A long time.

A: [Impatiently] Anyway, all of that is scarce here.

Z: All of what?

B: We have been trying to say it so that you understand. We have been trying to say it for a very long time. But "say" is not the word. Even "we" is not the word.

A: Something like that.

B: But there was that time when you were asking what it was that made those flowers talk on your street. Remember? In such a way that you could hear them? Remember you were asking us about that?

Z: [Standing, facing the voices expectantly.]

A: And all of your energy put into us.

B: But now what? What are you going to do now, with all that feeling?

III

listening to the travelling
flowers
the electronic age is a rose
roses are electricity
are
Voices.

—etel adnan

THEN NOTHING

Since we brought that rock home from the canyon
I keep seeing the girl who stirs sometimes, standing in there,
working at something, it looks like,
in the brush of her mind.
My own one's age, six or seven.
All the times she placed tiny things,
rips of paper, stones, in a row,
talking to herself. I place her
wondering there beside the wonder
of this girl, first hidden,
then risen into view
working on judgments in the already
of her mind's bright breath.

Though I have been without a story
for two years now, how near I feel her story.
Her brothers off to school, reaching so far now
that the sound of their laughter is almost
a hallucination, and in one world she is pouring grain
but really, she is placing the red words, one by one,
into the sumac, into the pomegranate for sleep there,
and how near I feel her story makes me wonder for
these words inside my head. Feeling she put them there.

Then what, when done with all the red then done
with all the milk, all
those little mouths will do?
Fused as they are in me,
in little thoughts and halts
whether I grow lean or more?

When finally I lose this form, this way to music,
the red she put inside of me
will be one flare

then nothing. After.

flower

in what you are
is there such thing
as dreaming
or fear
the sudden shock
of birds
a message
are you one
or am i
and the storms
their drums opening
your smile
your silver tooth
of dew
is there laughing
like the one
when the girl
lifts her face
i am always rushing
and you
somewhat still
beside the wall of stones
like a station of trains
or a large post office
where outside
people wait
in lines
for typists to type
resumés and
applications
and letters of who
was born
and who will
not go but

will stay
all through
the war
it seems
you know
so much there
with your field
getting older
with the rain
running through you
your life in one place
your little chair
of dirt upon
which you stand
orphic secret
with fog
is it through you
that the buried grow
a second communication
please show us to that well then
here are three more children
flower whose back
we lay the broken voice against
in rest when we are nothing left
and you carry us still
my flower

MY POEM

Hers now. Hers bare. The utter.

—Theresa Hak Kyung Cha

as a dream, open
as a door, mud

as a voice, shorn of flowers,
houred, low

as a daughter, an empty plate

and bread, torn of life

and a clock, one broken hand

a siren i was long without

a fly

from the dish of a hundred minnows,
i took one

where the birds go i am ignorant, beyond
the generalizations

as bougainvillea, mouths
of mothers

as basil flower, nearer the listening

as mountain i have failed

as a sister, i am burrs
a bell around the neck
of one far sheep

as a pigeon, i am religious
as religion, i am fire

as tears, the prickly pear
as stone, pure feeling

and a grave i will be without
as a sound a voice a candle

GLASS VOICE

The music teacher from seventh grade.
Not her name, but her hair.
Oak-colored, European, half-austere.

And how she had us all take turns going into her classroom
to sing.

And she told us, like a reverend with her wooden voice, what we
were. Alto, soprano.

One by one my friends floated back
having been anointed. Their diaphanous, soprano voices
smoothed onto their faces with the baby hairs and Vaseline.
Ripertonian pink. Sugarine. The angel in her ice cream.

-

To be songful and unobtrusive.

To be a mouse with my wooden stool and violin.

How difficult to think about it now, what I wanted.

But when I walked out of that room, the heavy stone had been set
in my hand.

What are you? they crowded around my difference.

Other things: my spotted tongue, my splitted ears and name.

-

In the harmonies I strayed and slid from pitch to pitch,
and this was proof to me of how I did not have a root
or home.

If I had been someone else it would have pleased me to be so
errant, slippery, loose. But being who I was
I worried not to keep the course,
to be so weak and influenced such that
I could not keep my part.

-

As a child, I sat in the high chair while
the doctor scraped my ears. Post-surgery.
It was from my ears that I first bled.

So that for many years I thought the work was to hear
my own voice

through all the language in the world

but hear only the light of

-

broken dust of bottle in the street, scratch of a stiffened broom. The people step around it talking into phones, holding leashes or the hands of their children. From the fire escape someone calls down to two women who have set up a tiny table and are eating one watermelon between them in the middle of the barricaded street.

Gold bangles on one arm, pigeons, the grey and terrible exhaust off the Mister Softee truck.

And when it comes through it is not mine.

*
^

be the dark shapely matter
buried beneath perhaps the
mountain but more generally
just underground the
mitochondrial memory
of the heart

NEVER COULD I BE WITHOUT YOU
I THOUGHT WE HAD MORE TIME

it used to be you called
my attention to
the bottlebrush
it used to be i put my hand
out & could speak to dogs
some sense some practice
buried now i am trying to
unearth it potatoes & wool
snow in my eyes why is it
that when
i close them
the first body i imagine
inside my own is not
blood & nerves
but my beloveds
their skin organs
skeletal structures
& nervous systems
are always that to which
i am awake awake
blessings to them
quiet x amen

in piñones they said
quiet because we were
on sacred ground & they
wanted us to take it in allí
está el camino por a dentro
that those who moved
between the plantations
& the community
of cimarrones took
when she was a little girl
she said she remembers
walking one path & hearing
the drums still calling
to each other in the mangles
we are being observed
we are strangers & something
is wondering whether or not
it is safe to reveal itself

i was closer many years
a whole lifetime back
then when i woke up
& could understand
that the stars were
somehow talking
above me i woke to
them & was on the edge
of hearing the transmission
of their vocalizations
in a language that i knew
was language & not one
i knew but that said
there were mysteries
through which information
crossed & like you
i was jagged with sisters
rock & dark a descendant

of space & that one day
it would be me too
the bats flew inside

NETSELA

I am 44 when I meet
my father's mother's goddaughter,
an old woman herself now,
at my cousin's wedding.

I did not meet my grandmother,
but she sent this for me
when I was little, I say,
pulling one small length of cloud
lined with burning stars
from my bag & she takes
the netsela in her hands.

This grief she whimpers, she coos
with small, dear tears in her eyes to touch it.

It occurs to me that her loss of my grandmother is differently
more real than mine. She knew her voice, her faces, & feelings.
What my grandmother touched in her memory was connected
to an intricate world of other ones & things within which this
woman grew. Saying any one of their names might be like lifting
a candle to see the contours of an old room, the faces on its walls.

Her eyes are still wet, &,
worried that something of her cries
for me & my children, I say,
But it is okay, okay. It is my daughter's now.
See, we wear her on our shoulders.
See, we wear her on our heads.

We knew

There were people with us there where faces blur
people in us there
whose hands grip her hat and the walking stick he rows
us down that river also our people
in a calabash skirt

We knew there were people with us
dreaming inside the stones
who left our mouths as horses stroked with the light

And so mine too would find me

> Once, just a few weeks after my love my love
> (I am touching my throat)
>
> he said to me at that fountain near La Caleta
> that he didn't see the point in us continuing on
> unceremoniously just like that
> I was so hurt so brokenboned of heart because
> he was for me a kind of psychic love
> and plain like that he said I don't see the point
> So for days I slept all day until that little bird
> flew into my room and landed on my foot
> I screamed and scared so much away with that jolt
> Those years were full of messages
> How that bird woke me
> in a kind of existential way
> That's when once just a few weeks later
> I ran down
> the long tear of a mountain
> and felt that elder pass me over in the rain
> to the younger one with the painted nails I was so
> surprised that I was being passed from
> an elder to an ancestor who had died younger
> and whose nails were so red

The elder said, *She is with you now*

No such thing as alone
No such thing as done or a name or free

cross *

this spectrum of breath & she,

the smaller fervors now,

a flash of secret, particulate power

maybe mostly ether, mostly

outside of pain now,

as windows, clover, rain.

Molecular, unseen,

hidden in the green of

the roses sharp with stars

over our shoulders as we are

children, learning to whistle, & then,

the children, they are ours,

made up of so much we cannot hear,

so much that does not speak *to us*

Yet Voice. Of the procession of ants.

Of the palm leaves resting on

the closely-shaven heads of schoolgirls.

Of the ocean material

& the neighbor stones

& the bed & the sheets

upon which a heart once

finished. Rest now, live one,

the clouds are always changing shape.

Touch touch, live one.

Everywhere is tear.

"And learn to imitate

her language there."

**This final quote is the fourteenth line of Phillis Wheatley Peters' "On the Death of a Young lady Age Five..."*

FOR A.

We hoped we would grow old still calling each other
and asking advice and remembering.

Saying everything plain, knowing where the other's heart is.

I wanted to be someone
who knew what questions to ask of her now
or how to go on in real friendship, listening.

What to say instead of standing
emptily in the line as her song spilled all over the store.

There is a recording of a poet reading her poem
about the porcelain in the desert and the fire,
and this moment when I think that I can see
an astonishment surge inside her.
She very briefly smiles.
Something physical and private and real.

The dream I'll leave for spokenness,
but that I saw A. briefly in the meridian, hanging photographs
from a tree in a future that extended and was mysterious.

It was a profound comfort to see her so happy.
Her soft, bare feet and red cotton dress.

Though I would not find her every time in this world,
to wonder what she would be tomorrow,
to know that she goes on.

after Nile Born, Ana Mendieta

I was so young I was the blood
still in my ears. I was so small
I was small as a kitchen cabinet
& watched the old mother at the window
on her knees, her back to me but
the palm of her one foot, brightdark
with henna, its shoulders
& waist where the arch was,
then the plumpness of the lower part
atop five legs or little, reddish eggs.
Eyeless, it faced me, & was my company
waiting for my parent to get off work.
I cannot recall the old mother's face, her name,
but the smooth slope of netsela makes her
sometimes a snowcovered hill,
or a cloud I witness briefly.

///

I wrote: "I cannot recall." Then waited
three days. I think I see
her eyes now. Wet, dark petals.
Her eyebrows are barely there.
On her forehead is the green, fading cross.
It is the green of tears, the green of flies.
They pollinate me with memory.

o

I am listening through Mendieta
for the silences of silt. The quiet
of some sentences with their
dark eyelashes bring me closer
to this scene. The quiet of this
mother's foot, my companion

for those hours, it is like the quiet of
the window, a page of world,
through which she listens.
What is she thinking? What does she
perceive? Maybe her children
alive & sleeping on the road
to Sudan. Maybe I have projected.
But it is possible. There is
something real of their crumbs,
their hair & dust. Here, fly,
take this. Carry this.

after Sin título (Sikán con chivo), Belkis Ayón

Almost a year, I carried
a xerox of Belkis Ayón's
collagraph of Sikán walking away
con el chivo in her arms,
perpetually pregnant with a fish,
looking over her shoulder, receding into
the waters of death flecked
with other fishes, all, to me,
sacred. I brought the xerox
with me up to Stockbridge-Munsee homeland,
where I microwaved & taught for
one semester. I was reading
Jennifer L. Morgan's *Laboring Women,*
recommended to me by Heidi,
& thinking about Belkis Ayón's work
with Sikán's story so that part
of what I began to see in the image
of pregnant Sikán carrying the killed goat
in her arms toward a realm of
other life had something to do
with Morgan's work with
the slaveowners' application of
the term "increase" not only to
nonhuman animals but also to
African women (*Laboring Women,* 83)
as a way of attempting to write our futures
into property & law. I begin to see
that perhaps every figure
in this collagraph is, in the story,
marked to be killed or used, or
to be proximate, to be the one
whose beloved is to be killed
or used. A sacrifice salvaging
the sacrificed, which is how
I understand the amulet she wears to be

a pre-sacrifice version of herself
& her little goat of jesus.
With the dead in her arms,
what did that image ward,
why does she wear it
still? But feel I lack
a way of seeing faithfully.

By the green river in that town,
fearing my babies might fall
from the high bed onto the concrete
floor in sleep, I slept on a mattress
on the floor with my two
while R. stayed back home
to work & took a bus up on
the weekends. I was paid well.
It was a time to study.
But with the kids so little
& so little reliable childcare,
every week was fingers crossed.
I brought the image of Sikán
to my office & studied it for long
stretches, longer than I looked out
of the window. Her arms cloaked
with medieval scales & the mother/baby
amulet, both their heads made
in brightless aura. Then I went back home.

The river moving, remembering past us
through the freezing nights where I
edged the question of her fictional
mouthlessness but closed on facts
that cannot be survived.

I have seen mothers go on mothering
their violated children even after death,
worrying for their empty bellies, choosing

their burial clothes, kissing kissing kissing
what is left, flying to them in the past
to throw a flower at their feet
when they were going with the others
to school.

Death does not kill relation.

To have a mother
like this to come for you,
to carry you dead
into the veil of fishes,
who would not let
you go.

IV

You Are Who I Love

1/2017 – 1/2025

You, selling roses out of a silver grocery cart

You, in the park, feeding the pigeons
You cheering for the bees

You with cats in your voice in the morning, feeding cats

You protecting the river   You are who I love
delivering the babies, nursing the sick

You with henna on your feet and a gold star in your nose

You taking your medicine, reading the magazines

You looking into the faces of the young people as they pass, smiling and saying, *Alright!* which, they know it, means *I see you, Family. I love you. Keep on.*

You dancing in the kitchen, on the sidewalk, in the subway
waiting for the train   because Stevie Wonder, Héctor Lavoe,
La Lupe

You stirring the pot of beans, you washing your father's feet

You are who I love, you
reciting Darwish, then June

Feeding your heart, teaching your parents how to do
The Dougie, counting to 10, reading your patients' charts

You are who I love, standing in line for water, stocking
the food pantries, making a meal

You, in the cold, unraveling your blanket to make hats
for the heads of children

You are who I love, flooding the streets, arriving on buses, on
trains, in cars, by foot to stand in the January streets against
the cold and brutal offices saying:
YOUR CRUELTY DOES NOT SPEAK FOR ME

You are who I love, you struggling to see

You struggling to love or find a question,
alive with refusal, standing in the wind, you, salvaging
the umbrellas, graduating from school,
wearing holes in your shoes

You are who I love
weeping or touching the faces of the weeping

You, Violeta Parra, grateful for the alphabet,
for sound, singing toward us in the dream

You butterflies
You carrying your brother home

Sharing your water, sharing your potatoes and greens

You who did and did not survive
You who cleaned the kitchens
You who built the railroad tracks and roads
You who replanted the trees, listening to the work of squirrels
and birds, you are who I love

You whose blood was taken, whose hands and lives were taken,
with or without your saying *Yes, I mean to give*
You are who I love

You who the borders crossed
You whose fires
You decent with rage, so in love with the earth
You writing poems alongside children

You cactus, water, sparrow, crow   You, my elder
You are who I love,
summoning the courage, making the cobbler,

getting the blood drawn, sharing the difficult news, you always
planting the marigolds, learning to walk wherever you are,
learning to read wherever you are,
                                        you baking the bread,
you come to me in dreams, you kissing the faces of your dead
wherever you are, speaking to your children in your mother's
languages, tootsing the birds

You are who I love, behind the library desk,
leaving who might kill you, crying with the love songs,
polishing your shoes, lighting the candles,
getting through your first day despite the
whisperers sniping fail fail fail

You are who I love, you who beat and did not beat the odds, you
who knows that any good thing you have is the result of
someone else's sacrifice, work, you who fights for reparations

You are who I love whose face is saying *Selam*,
whose name is talking with the leaves

You are who I love, singing Leonard Cohen to the snow
with glitter on your face, wearing
a kilt and violet lipstick

You are who I love, sighing in your sleep

You, playing drums in the procession, feeding the chickens
and humming as you hem the skirt

You sharpening the pencil,
You writing the poem about the loneliness of the astronaut

You wanting to listen,
You trying to be so still

You are who I love, mothering the dogs, standing with horses,
pledging your allegiance to the grass

You in brightness and in darkness, throwing your head back as
you laugh, kissing your hand

You carrying the berbere from the mill, and the tears
of the trees of the olives you belong to
                    You braiding your child's hair

You are who I love, crossing the desert
and trying to cross the desert

You are who I love, working the shifts
to buy books, rice, tomatoes,
bathing your children as you listen to the lecture,
heating the kitchen with the oven, up early, up late

You are who I love, learning English, learning Spanish,
drawing flowers on your hand with a ballpoint pen, taking the
bus home

          I love your working heart,
how each of its gestures, tiny or big, stand beside my own agony,
building a forest there

You carrying the signs, packing the lunches, with the rain on
your face
                    You at the edges and shores, in the rooms of quiet,
in the rooms of shouting, saying "no"
                                        and each of us looking out from

the gorgeous sliver of our lives at all, finding ourselves here, witnesses to each other's tenderness, which, this moment, is fury, is rage, which, this moment, is another way of saying *You are who I love*
You are who I love   You and you and you are who

GREEN OF ALL HEADS LEFT OPEN AT THE TOP

-- in the presence of -- the trees -- i carry my sorrows below --
their branches -- "probably always" i overhear R. say --

to the children -- the air -- full of memory -- where --
where have you been? -- trying -- pebbles of words --

i am learning to lift -- my voice -- like a flower -- in --
a field of flowers -- sometimes, i hear you -- all heads

left open at the top -- through mine i wonder -- now

THIS ANIMAL

Nearly done. Hunched against
the curb's low wall. Poisoned,
pained into frantic stillness.

By what do I feel she is a woman rat
Her stoic, outcast labor.
Her injury among the trash and cups and carts.

Like any of us, maybe she was cared for
in the beginning of her life
and then was left, will not recover
the ones to whom she belonged.

Not last, not less.
Just sad, lone, ash.

Just that where are her people.

Somehow my mind is with her—scattered, stray
the small tongue of this animal

whose world this was

THE DOG

I.

Groan out that great eye, all shouting shat

& dribbled, growing larger.

The midwives used their cloths

To shine my mirror.

Across two years the babies fell, first one

Then the other out of that obsidian, my exhalations.

Once with wires the other all free,

Each of them spinning knots in their cords.

I feared & feared, one for each one.

I had read somewhere small lines of Ingrian history

Describing a tradition of opening all the braids & knots

Of a person birthing in order to assist

With her effacement. I grew effaced. Each eye carried one wolf

& the memory came back to me from

When I worked in Bluefields one summer

Under the guidance of Doña Nidia,

Interviewing Black women community leaders

For an oral history,

& in my months there with her learning,

I sometimes passed a table,

On my way to the office, a table manned by men who sold

Glass beads & other things I can't remember now,

But what I remember most are the dark hay-colored pelts

The color of dark hay-colored dogs,

Painted with black markings from what seemed to me to be

Shoe polish, in stripes, & when I finally asked

The men said they were the pelts of women

Who disguised themselves as wild animals

(But did they say dogs or is that just

What comes to me now?) to do their wandering & work.

& sometimes these women shed their pelts in some secret place

To become human women again

& these men stole them which meant the women could not return

To them & that in these pelts was some of the power.

They could be bought. Though I don't remember

The men at the table

Expressing any interest in selling them to me,

Who knows why I think of this now except for

Ten years I have been inside the dog.

The night when that first labor was done

I stood at the mirror aberrating, matted,

& from one flat eye heard jackal jackal.

Who walked the perimeter, who led the dead,

Our ankles spotted with blood. & stomach's

Black roses off of which our babies fed. Again

Contracting, purple as a lens. Subject.

Soundbroken. Dispersed onto every limb. I am not freen.

Could not lay down this skin.

II.
In one beginning.

A roving eye, I took my notes & watched for symptoms.

The offices hummed with ugly, off-white energy

& large beige computers. Antiseptic light.

Nothing was wild.

I said my name to a person on the other side of the glass.

I signed my forms with a pen kept on a cold, silver leash.

Drone of lights. But that the heart is barking.

III.

for you

There is a beginning before all of this

Which does not begin with the hospital or even grandmother.

As a child, I wanted to be able to lay the egg,

To be the mother of a chick & steward it with my heat.

Later the science & pleasures, later the blood

& where to bury the placenta.

How I tried to open the knots in my closed eyes.

I opened these knots & filled my milk

With trees. The cleft trees I passed my body through,

I crawled below their roots. I closed my eyes

& filled ourselves with dog. The dog of my womanhood.

The dogs of the battles

Of births. The dog of the weighing of the heart.

Dog who fed children. Its long milk run

All through our middle. The land dreams

Quartz. Dreaming, we have become its parallel.

I take my place in line to come back.

Through the milk, closed eyes inside of eyes,

runs the sentence: We are born onto the bareness of the earth

Thousands of ways. La lei lo lai, la lei lo lei.

I feel the mothers hurry to add to my milk (for you):

A basket, coffee, shiro, & hay.

AWAKEN YOUR WILL

Many years from now, the birds screamed
To each other in the lessening night
And something shook me from the dream
Of horses. Before I could close,
One had run out into the dry, hushed bed
Of the river whose bank
We laid our sleeping bags beside
Following the teacher's printed map.
The horse made a sound,
His left eye shone purple
Against the flashlight light.
How close, its hooves.
Years from now, but it is
Calling to me
Like a so cket
Of sight:
Awaken your will
As when everyone was here.

X

With the babies drinking from me
I tried to get my head right with dirt,
to flower, to be touched by the sun,
by dark, to hear that bembé bell
or return to the backroom of the botánica
off of Seventeenth, I think, where Mom
finally found the cat's claw.
So help one Read. So help one See.
—to make one black X on the ground
& leave the sentence a little open. & then fly.
To learn some of the syllables of the water.
I would see who was my brother, my sister down there.
In that old recurring dream from childhood
it was another life reaching through
over such churning ocean where they separated
the females from males so then, like now,
we were apart, & there was
no father with you physically,
but in the smallest bone of your ear
lived the memory of laughing with him
as children, & the cousins all around,
& somewhere else our elders
plotted fire for the disappeared.

Cover the path with Black and Red.
Bury in our heads what we
find of our dead.

MAKING HER BODY BED

Instinctively I face
the brown doll up
to see the day
but this day
it is an imposition so
turn her back over & feel
that after so many years
I finally know
what a doll is for.
Like, yeah, if I cannot lay
all day in the dream/dirt
then maybe the doll can for me.
A way to with the action
write a horizon at rest
in the house
as I'd go going
about my day.
I could do this with stones, with twigs.
I could do this with words like Voice
Voice Voice, to open doors,
to let the dream's dark out
in the morning
as an animal.
To watch its needful run.
From the window I can see it
dart at first, then rub its
back across the grass,
freeing itself in the bushes,
feeding off of tree plums.
I turn away my attention
so she is talking in her head in peace,
unobserved, growing muscles in her voice,
& her legs, how strong
she runs off out
of rooms we made

X

un templo que nos habla y no nos nombra
—Homero Aridjis

For months we made so much information
passing back and forth through us,
silence striated with cells, subterranean,
an idea I am getting at for how the hair goes grey
and there is birth, and death,
and what is unnameable about us
exists, hawthorne, sunlight.
So when the nurse held up our cord
because it was a shining knot,
we had already been each other's
for at least a single star.
It is not true who says you don't remember.
From a distance I could feel you
looking down something like a long dirt road,
waving me off, knowing or
not knowing that would be it.
Should I call you adcy, mma.
Should I call you grandmother.
Black of the green leaf, black of the pot.
How all our lives so far were touched with them,
and now a veil of black roses across both our stomachs.
The nurse named our dogeyes supernumerary,
summoning our constellation, and suddenly
milk murmuring in the flowers.
"un templo que nos habla y no nos nombra"
It was you, it was you
from the sky all those times ago
who threw that ladder down,
to us! And now, and now,
a face to touch. Our love
and blackest heart,
our true, whose eye of voices...

even when we did,
we could not name you.

WASHING THE MIRROR

Years ago I stayed
two hundred yards from an Italian castle
at a residency for artists where for six weeks I slept
in a small house on a hill
at the end of a groundstone path,
the Dianas and their stoic, crying
cypresses.

It was me and M.

There was an iron gate between us and the castle
and we passed through it on our way to the library
and to eat with the others.

That season of wind, the gate was always locking us out
and we each felt different ways about it.

There were also persimmons which shone on us
their own light, and the cross still there from when
the priest had earlier blessed the fields.
The strained, dry necks of sunflowers
with their heavy, areolic eyes that seemed to see
what passed that road to Gubbio
dotted with old plastic chairs
and immigrant women hired for sex
by the citizen truckers under
the forest cover.

On a walk, I found a mattress
and asked about it. Or my memory
is wrong and someone told me
that there were mattresses
and so vividly I see one now,
in a clearing of light

and wood and stains
and leaves.

On another walk
I heard those hunters shooting
and did not have any colorful hat
so tried to go to where the path
was most unhidden and wide.

I worried that I did not know the signs
for aggression or violence or pity
so that in order to begin
I had to break a spell to throw what I held
away from me.

I lit the candles and said the names.
I greeted the view from every window
but in my room the mirror, too,
watched me stonily so I carried
it out to wash it with the sky
for hours one day and, I think,
another day. To rinse from it
its visions and blow its candles dry.
I placed it face up to the clouds
who fled in families above
and was surprised to see it open
its mouth so widely and thought
it must have been inside
for very long.

Its strange, white moan
so hungry, so animaline.

It had no teeth.
No shoes.
No hair.

And was just a single, oval
throat of light.

I am looking back
from the future and think of it
as I try to find
my sight. To burn from me what
I do not need, I open.
            I open my vaginamind   to the sun

NOTES

"December" emerges on Coast Miwok, Huimen land.

Page 13: Suzanne Césaire's words are from her 1942 "Malaise d'une civilisation," translated by Keith L. Walker in *The Great Camouflage* as: "*Surrender to self, to the seasons, to the moon, to the more or less long day. Fruit harvest. And always and everywhere in the slightest manifestations, the primacy of the plant, the plant trampled underfoot but still alive, dead but reviving, the plant free...*"

Page 13: Roger Reeves' words here are from his poem "Children Listen" from *Best Barbarian*.

"Funeral" is written in astonished and dearest memory of my dad, Girmay Keleta, and his dear friend Solomon Kebede. Devoted to the cause of Eritrean independence and to their communities, each of them organized beautifully, formidably, joyfully toward that effort. My childhood was saturated with this dream. When I look back, I am astonished to think about how young they were, and what they survived. And what life they made with their lives. And how impossible it is to reconcile the facts of their lives (my dad had survived a massive stroke five years prior) with the tragedy of their deaths—they were killed when struck by a car while crossing the street. As was true of birthing my children and later sending them to school, my father's death brought me into a greater and different understanding of the state's devaluation of life and its industries of death. This text grows out of this impossibility.

Page 65: Etel Adnan's words are from "The Spring Flowers Own" found in *The Spring Flowers Own & The Manifestations of the Voyage.*

"My Poem": Includes an epigraph from Theresa Hak Kyung Cha's *Dictee.*

" * "

^ : During the Cumbre Afro 2023 at la UPR-Río Piedras, Mayra Santos-Febres arranged for participants to visit the mangroves stewarded by COPI (Corporación Piñones Se Integra). Oriented by the stewards' care for, and long relationship with, the mangroves, and their expectation that we attune ourselves to the presences of the forest, this poem began to emerge. El camino por a dentro led to the bosque but also to memory.

"You Are Who I Love": I was invited by Sarah Browning at Split This Rock to contribute to a chorus of poems to be released around the 2017 inauguration. Months before that, in the vile climate of the presidential elections in the U.S., I had come upon two children—maybe 11 or 12, joyous, alive, Black—on their bikes, selling water beneath the LIRR on Atlantic somewhere in Bed-Stuy, Brooklyn. My own child was about one and a half, much younger than them, which contributed to the sense of awe I felt to see these children so at ease in themselves. Their collaboration, their shouts and togetherness and laughter. For me a poem usually becomes in the dreaming that happens in the material of language. But this poem happened outside of writing it. The poem was the work of turning my attention toward the efforts of the beautiful others trying to Live! in the Gwendolynian way. It was the work of turning toward their (our) aliveness and their (our) lives. I heard myself say inside myself but to those children: YOU are who I love. I was a body thrummed by the languages of others—Mahmoud Darwish, June Jordan, Audre Lorde, Adrienne Rich—and so there are those echoes here. Over the course of months, the poem became. It continues to become.

"X" on page 110: the Homero Aridjis epigraph is from *Poemas Solares Solar Poems*. Translated differently in his book, I hear "un templo que nos habla y no nos nombra" as "a temple that speaks to us and does not name us.

Whose work touched open my head: Kamau Brathwaite, June Jordan, Teberh Tesfahuney, Gwendolyn Brooks, Belkis Ayón, Paul Celan, Suzanne Césaire, Etel Adnan, Agnes Martin, Mahmoud Darwish, Theresa Hak Kyung Cha, Jean Valentine, Lucille Clifton.

ACKNOWLEDGMENTS

Thank you to the editors, curators, and staff of the following publications and projects in which versions of these poems first appeared:

Academy of American Poets, Poem-a-Day series: "Ceremony for Remembering the Doorless World" and "[*When I come home they rush to me, the flies...*]";

e-flux: "We knew";

MoMA Poetry Project: "*after Nile Born, Ana Mendieta*";

The Poetry Review: " * ";
^

The Quarry, Split This Rock: "You Are Who I Love";

Wheatley at 250: "cross."

I made so much of this work in the underground of change and griefs, and in the abundances and challenge of love and children and all kinds of collectives. Thank you to my family, dear friends, neighbors, and collaborators in work and study, for your root and challenge, your discipline and care, your unruly example and vast belief. Thank you for keeping us close in spirit, joy, and question. In particular, and none of this without: Lisa, Marina, Mendi, Simone, Zeynep, Erynn, Angel, Shira, 570, Erin, Anna, Alysia, Nell, Ellie, Deb G. Michele. Deb, Cynthia, Cheryl, Yesenia, Kathy, Marta Lucía, Roberto, Rachel, Claudia, Umniya, Rigoberto. Trace, Cindy, Sarah, Jasmine, Joël, Thiahera, Moncho, Haydil, Sokunthary, Sébastien. Poets with whom all the workshops. Aisha, whose love and question *–do you have something?* – I feel across the years. Ellen, whose love and question *–do you have something?* – I also feel across the years. Claire, Ama: inviting me into two critical collaborations and so into paper, scissors, glue, and intuition. Patrick and Ross: marrow language across, whose listening makes it more possible to sound with what is quietest. Amina: whose belief is love. Thanks to Catherine Barnett, for your questions and attention. Ruth Worrede: for more language. My first teachers: Aida Heredia, Elizabeth Alexander, Nikky Finney, Kamau Brathwaite, Martín Espada, Blanche McCrary Boyd, Charles O. Hartman, Reggie Flood. Mom, whose prayers were language alive. Dad, whose commitments and questions move me toward—.

I give thanks to the contributors to *So We Can Know* who perhaps cannot imagine how profoundly I continue to learn from their fierce, capacious work. My true thanks to the editorial board of the African Poetry Book Fund, Kwame Dawes and Matthew Shenoda in particular, whose vision of what we can do and how we can be continues to open the paths. I feel this way, too, about Beth Loffreda. Thank you. Gratitude to the curators and participants of Loophole of Retreat, as well as to Suhaly Bautista-Carolina who invited me to write poems toward *Hear Me Now,* the Black potters of Old Edgefield, South Carolina exhibit at The Met. Gratitude to the Clifton family, the Clifton House, Joël Diaz, Bernard Schwartz, Valentina Améstica, Ellen Hagan, and Ricardo Maldonado whose support and collaboration with other work helped me to more clearly feel what this was. Thank you to Jess Fisher for bringing me to Williams where so much of this study – a fern's fist – began to open, and to Jess, Mérida, and Nelly for wrapping us up in your welcome. Christian Campbell whose invitation to participate in a celebration for wondrous Kamau Brathwaite at the World Voices Festival gifted me with the chance to think about Brathwaite, presence, and teaching. This articulation put me in deeper touch with certain mysteries of feeling and relation that I would soon come to need. Thank you to Civitella Ranieri, the June Jordan Fellowship, and the American Academy of Arts and Letters for support which nourished these poems. I am profoundly moved that the brilliant Harold Meltzer set "You Are Who I Love" with an original composition for Sandbox Percussion and The Crossing.

Peter, thank you for your incredible belief, trust, and support. Thank you to everyone at BOA.

Thank you for ground: Mumzie, Baba Gary, Damian, Sabine & family, Nadia & family, Bereket & family, Paola, Levi, Aster.

Rassan, earth in my book, steadiness of heart, whose seeking deepens mine. Alem, Ezmi: my loves, my mysteries. Nayeli, Yosef, Ariana, Mom: I touch my head to yours and in these worlds give thanks to all that would *hear* it.

Kamilah Aisha Moon, ever with you. Dad, ever with you.

ABOUT THE AUTHOR

Aracelis Girmay is a poet and editor. Her poems and essays have been published widely and can be found in *e-flux*, *The Paris Review* online, and *The Poetry Review*. Girmay was named a finalist for the Neustadt International Prize for Literature and was a recipient of the Whiting Award. Her books have been named finalists for the National Book Critics Circle Award and the Hurston/Wright Legacy Award. Girmay is on the editorial board of the African Poetry Book Fund. *GREEN OF ALL HEADS* is her fourth full-length collection. She lives in the East Bay and teaches at Stanford University.

BOA Editions, Ltd. American Poets Continuum Series

No. 1 *The Fuhrer Bunker: A Cycle of Poems in Progress*
W. D. Snodgrass

No. 2 *She*
M. L. Rosenthal

No. 3 *Living With Distance*
Ralph J. Mills, Jr.

No. 4 *Not Just Any Death*
Michael Waters

No. 5 *That Was Then: New and Selected Poems*
Isabella Gardner

No. 6 *Things That Happen Where There Aren't Any People*
William Stafford

No. 7 *The Bridge of Change: Poems 1974–1980*
John Logan

No. 8 *Signatures*
Joseph Stroud

No. 9 *People Live Here: Selected Poems 1949–1983*
Louis Simpson

No. 10 *Yin*
Carolyn Kizer

No. 11 *Duhamel: Ideas of Order in Little Canada*
Bill Tremblay

No. 12 *Seeing It Was So*
Anthony Piccione

No. 13 *Hyam Plutzik: The Collected Poems*

No. 14 *Good Woman: Poems and a Memoir 1969–1980*
Lucille Clifton

No. 15 *Next: New Poems*
Lucille Clifton

No. 16 *Roxa: Voices of the Culver Family*
William B. Patrick

No. 17 *John Logan: The Collected Poems*

No. 18 *Isabella Gardner: The Collected Poems*

No. 19 *The Sunken Lightship*
Peter Makuck

No. 20 *The City in Which I Love You*
Li-Young Lee

No. 21 *Quilting: Poems 1987–1990*
Lucille Clifton

No. 22 *John Logan: The Collected Fiction*

No. 23 *Shenandoah and Other Verse Plays*
Delmore Schwartz

No. 24 *Nobody Lives on Arthur Godfrey Boulevard*
Gerald Costanzo

No. 25 *The Book of Names: New and Selected Poems*
Barton Sutter

No. 26 *Each in His Season*
W. D. Snodgrass

No. 27 *Wordworks: Poems Selected and New*
Richard Kostelanetz

No. 28 *What We Carry*
Dorianne Laux

No. 29 *Red Suitcase*
Naomi Shihab Nye

No. 30 *Song*
Brigit Pegeen Kelly

No. 31 *The Fuehrer Bunker: The Complete Cycle*
W. D. Snodgrass

No. 32 *For the Kingdom*
Anthony Piccione

No. 33 *The Quicken Tree*
Bill Knott

No. 34 *These Upraised Hands*
William B. Patrick

No. 35 *Crazy Horse in Stillness*
William Heyen

No. 36 *Quick, Now, Always*
Mark Irwin

No. 37 *I Have Tasted the Apple*
Mary Crow

No. 38 *The Terrible Stories*
Lucille Clifton

No. 39 *The Heat of Arrivals*
Ray Gonzalez

No. 40 *Jimmy & Rita*
Kim Addonizio

No. 41 *Green Ash, Red Maple, Black Gum*
Michael Waters

No. 42 *Against Distance*
Peter Makuck

No. 43 *The Night Path*
Laurie Kutchins

No. 44 *Radiography*
Bruce Bond

No. 45 *At My Ease: Uncollected Poems of the Fifties and Sixties*
David Ignatow

No. 46 *Trillium*
Richard Foerster

No. 47 *Fuel*
Naomi Shihab Nye

No. 48 *Gratitude*
Sam Hamill

No. 49 *Diana, Charles, & the Queen*
William Heyen

No. 50 *Plus Shipping*
Bob Hicok

No. 51 *Cabato Sentora*
Ray Gonzalez

No. 52 *We Didn't Come Here for This*
William B. Patrick

No. 53 *The Vandals*
Alan Michael Parker

No. 54 *To Get Here*
Wendy Mnookin

No. 55 *Living Is What I Wanted: Last Poems*
David Ignatow

No. 56 *Dusty Angel*
Michael Blumenthal

No. 57 *The Tiger Iris*
Joan Swift

No. 58 *White City*
Mark Irwin

No. 59 *Laugh at the End of the World: Collected Comic Poems 1969–1999*
Bill Knott

No. 60 *Blessing the Boats: New and Selected Poems: 1988–2000*
Lucille Clifton

No. 61 *Tell Me*
Kim Addonizio

No. 62 *Smoke*
Dorianne Laux

No. 63 *Parthenopi: New and Selected Poems*
Michael Waters

No. 64 *Rancho Notorious*
Richard Garcia

No. 65 *Jam*
Joe-Anne McLaughlin

No. 66 *A. Poulin, Jr. Selected Poems*
Edited, with an Introduction by Michael Waters

No. 67 *Small Gods of Grief*
Laure-Anne Bosselaar

No. 68 *Book of My Nights*
Li-Young Lee

No. 69 *Tulip Farms and Leper Colonies*
Charles Harper Webb

No. 70 *Double Going*
Richard Foerster

No. 71 *What He Took*
Wendy Mnookin

No. 72 *The Hawk Temple at Tierra Grande*
Ray Gonzalez

No. 73 *Mules of Love*
Ellen Bass

No. 74 *The Guests at the Gate*
Anthony Piccione

No. 75 *Dumb Luck*
Sam Hamill

No. 76 *Love Song with Motor Vehicles*
Alan Michael Parker

No. 77 *Life Watch*
Willis Barnstone

No. 78 *The Owner of the House: New Collected Poems 1940–2001*
Louis Simpson

No. 79 *Is*
Wayne Dodd

No. 80 *Late*
Cecilia Woloch

No. 81 *Precipitates*
Debra Kang Dean

No. 82 *The Orchard*
Brigit Pegeen Kelly

No. 83 *Bright Hunger*
Mark Irwin

No. 84 *Desire Lines: New and Selected Poems*
Lola Haskins

No. 85 *Curious Conduct*
Jeanne Marie Beaumont

No. 86 *Mercy*
Lucille Clifton

No. 87 *Model Homes*
Wayne Koestenbaum

No. 88 *Farewell to the Starlight in Whiskey*
Barton Sutter

No. 89 *Angels for the Burning*
David Mura

No. 90 *The Rooster's Wife*
Russell Edson

No. 91 *American Children*
Jim Simmerman

No. 92 *Postcards from the Interior*
Wyn Cooper

No. 93 *You & Yours*
Naomi Shihab Nye

No. 94 *Consideration of the Guitar: New and Selected Poems 1986–2005*
Ray Gonzalez

No. 95 *Off-Season in the Promised Land*
Peter Makuck

No. 96 *The Hoopoe's Crown*
Jacqueline Osherow

No. 97 *Not for Specialists: New and Selected Poems*
W. D. Snodgrass

No. 98 *Splendor*
Steve Kronen

No. 99 *Woman Crossing a Field*
Deena Linett

No. 100 *The Burning of Troy*
Richard Foerster

No. 101 *Darling Vulgarity*
Michael Waters

No. 102 *The Persistence of Objects*
Richard Garcia

No. 103 *Slope of the Child Everlasting*
Laurie Kutchins

No. 104 *Broken Hallelujahs*
Sean Thomas Dougherty

No. 105 *Peeping Tom's Cabin: Comic Verse 1928–2008*
X. J. Kennedy

No. 106 *Disclamor*
G.C. Waldrep

No. 107 *Encouragement for a Man Falling to His Death*
Christopher Kennedy

No. 108 *Sleeping with Houdini*
Nin Andrews

No. 109 *Nomina*
Karen Volkman

No. 110 *The Fortieth Day*
Kazim Ali

No. 111 *Elephants & Butterflies*
Alan Michael Parker

No. 112 *Voices*
Lucille Clifton

No. 113 *The Moon Makes Its Own Plea*
Wendy Mnookin

No. 114 *The Heaven-Sent Leaf*
Katy Lederer

No. 115 *Struggling Times*
Louis Simpson

No. 116 *And*
Michael Blumenthal

No. 117 *Carpathia*
Cecilia Woloch

No. 118 *Seasons of Lotus, Seasons of Bone*
Matthew Shenoda

No. 119 *Sharp Stars*
Sharon Bryan

No. 120 *Cool Auditor*
Ray Gonzalez

No. 121 *Long Lens: New and Selected Poems*
Peter Makuck

No. 122 *Chaos Is the New Calm*
Wyn Cooper

No. 123 *Diwata*
Barbara Jane Reyes

No. 124 *Burning of the Three Fires*
Jeanne Marie Beaumont

No. 125 *Sasha Sings the Laundry on the Line*
Sean Thomas Dougherty

No. 126 *Your Father on the Train of Ghosts*
G.C. Waldrep and John Gallaher

No. 127 *Ennui Prophet*
Christopher Kennedy

No. 128 *Transfer*
Naomi Shihab Nye

No. 129 *Gospel Night*
Michael Waters

No. 130 *The Hands of Strangers: Poems from the Nursing Home*
Janice N. Harrington

No. 131 *Kingdom Animalia*
Aracelis Girmay

No. 132 *True Faith*
Ira Sadoff

No. 133 *The Reindeer Camps and Other Poems*
Barton Sutter

No. 134 *The Collected Poems of Lucille Clifton: 1965–2010*

No. 135 *To Keep Love Blurry*
Craig Morgan Teicher

No. 136 *Theophobia*
Bruce Beasley

No. 137 *Refuge*
Adrie Kusserow

No. 138 *The Book of Goodbyes*
Jillian Weise

No. 139 *Birth Marks*
Jim Daniels

No. 140 *No Need of Sympathy*
Fleda Brown

No. 141 *There's a Box in the Garage You Can Beat with a Stick*
Michael Teig

No. 142 *The Keys to the Jail*
Keetje Kuipers

No. 143 *All You Ask for Is Longing: New and Selected Poems 1994–2014*
Sean Thomas Dougherty

No. 144 *Copia*
Erika Meitner

No. 145 *The Chair: Prose Poems*
Richard Garcia

No. 146 *In a Landscape*
John Gallaher

No. 147 *Fanny Says*
Nickole Brown

No. 148 *Why God Is a Woman*
Nin Andrews

No. 149 *Testament*
G.C. Waldrep

No. 150 *I'm No Longer Troubled by the Extravagance*
Rick Bursky

No. 151 *Antidote for Night*
Marsha de la O

No. 152 *Beautiful Wall*
Ray Gonzalez

No. 153 *the black maria*
Aracelis Girmay

No. 154 *Celestial Joyride*
Michael Waters

No. 155 *Whereso*
Karen Volkman

No. 156 *The Day's Last Light Reddens the Leaves of the Copper Beech*
Stephen Dobyns

No. 157 *The End of Pink*
Kathryn Nuernberger

No. 158 *Mandatory Evacuation*
Peter Makuck

No. 159 *Primitive: The Art and Life of Horace H. Pippin*
Janice N. Harrington

No. 160 *The Trembling Answers*
Craig Morgan Teicher

No. 161 *Bye-Bye Land*
Christian Barter

No. 162 *Sky Country*
Christine Kitano

No. 163 *All Soul Parts Returned*
Bruce Beasley

No. 164 *The Smoke of Horses*
Charles Rafferty

No. 165 *The Second O of Sorrow*
Sean Thomas Dougherty

No. 166 *Holy Moly Carry Me*
Erika Meitner

No. 167 *Clues from the Animal Kingdom*
Christopher Kennedy

No. 168 *Dresses from the Old Country*
Laura Read

No. 169 *In Country*
Hugh Martin

No. 170 *The Tiny Journalist*
Naomi Shihab Nye

No. 171 *All Its Charms*
Keetje Kuipers

No. 172 *Night Angler*
Geffrey Davis

No. 173 *The Human Half*
Deborah Brown

No. 174 *Cyborg Detective*
Jillian Weise

No. 175 *On the Shores of Welcome Home*
Bruce Weigl

No. 176 *Rue*
Kathryn Nuernberger

No. 177 *Let's Become a Ghost Story*
Rick Bursky

No. 178 *Year of the Dog*
Deborah Paredez

No. 179 *Brand New Spacesuit*
John Gallaher

No. 180 *How to Carry Water: Selected Poems of Lucille Clifton*
Edited, with an Introduction by Aracelis Girmay

No. 181 *Caw*
Michael Waters

No. 182 *Letters to a Young Brown Girl*
Barbara Jane Reyes

No. 183 *Mother Country*
Elana Bell

No. 184 *Welcome to Sonnetville, New Jersey*
Craig Morgan Teicher

No. 185 *I Am Not Trying to Hide My Hungers from the World*
Kendra DeColo

No. 186 *The Naomi Letters*
Rachel Mennies

No. 187 *Tenderness*
Derrick Austin

No. 188 *Ceive*
B.K. Fischer

No. 189 *Diamonds*
Camille Guthrie

No. 190 *A Cluster of Noisy Planets*
Charles Rafferty

No. 191 *Useful Junk*
Erika Meitner

No. 192 *Field Notes from the Flood Zone*
Heather Sellers

No. 193 *A Season in Hell with Rimbaud*
Dustin Pearson

No. 194 *Your Emergency Contact Has Experienced an Emergency*
Chen Chen

No. 195 *A Tinderbox in Three Acts*
Cynthia Dewi Oka

No. 196 *Little Mr. Prose Poem: Selected Poems of Russell Edson*
Edited by Craig Morgan Teicher

No. 197 *The Dug-Up Gun Museum*
Matt Donovan

No. 198 *Four in Hand*
Alicia Mountain

No. 199 *Buffalo Girl*
Jessica Q. Stark

No. 200 *Nomenclatures of Invisibility*
Mahtem Shiferraw

No. 201 *Flare, Corona*
Jeannine Hall Gailey

No. 202 *Death Prefers the Minor Keys*
Sean Thomas Dougherty

No. 203 *Desire Museum*
Danielle Deulen

No. 204 *Transitory*
Subhaga Crystal Bacon

No. 205 *Every Hard Sweetness*
Sheila Carter-Jones

No. 206 *Blue on a Blue Palette*
Lynne Thompson

No. 207 *One Wild Word Away*
Geffrey Davis

No. 208 *The Strange God Who Makes Us*
Christopher Kennedy

No. 209 *Our Splendid Failure to Do the Impossible*
Rebecca Lindenberg

No. 210 *Yard Show*
Janice N. Harrington

No. 211 *The Last Song of the World*
Joseph Fasano

No. 212 *Lonely Women Make Good Lovers*
Keetje Kuipers

No. 213 *jump the gun*
Jennie Malboeuf

No. 214 *Apostle of Desire*
Bruce Weigl

No. 215 *GREEN OF ALL HEADS*
Aracelis Girmay

COLOPHON

BOA Editions, Ltd., a nonprofit publisher of poetry and other literary works, fosters readership and appreciation of contemporary literature. By identifying, cultivating, and publishing both new and established poets and selecting authors of unique literary talent, BOA brings high-quality literature to the public.

Support for this effort comes from the sale of its publications, grant funding, and private donations.

*

The publication of this book is made possible, in part, by the special support of the following individuals:

Anonymous
Ralph Black & Susan Murphy
Angela Bonazinga & Catherine Lewis
Gwen Conners, *in memory of June Baker*
Chris Dahl, *in honor of Chuck Hertrick*
Jonathan Everitt
Bonnie Garner
James Hale
Kelly Hatton & Tom White
Chuck Hertrick & Joan Gerrity
Grant Holcomb
Teresa D. Johnson
Nora A. Jones
Joe & Dale Klein
Jack & Gail Langerak
Barbara Lovenheim, *in memory of John Lovenheim*
Joe McElveney
John & Judy Messenger
Dorrie Parini
Boo Poulin, *in memory of A. Poulin Jr.*
Michael Quattrone
Deborah Ronnen
John H. Schultz
Lynne Thompson
William Waddell & Linda Rubel
Michael Waters & Mihaela Moscaliuc